LEARN TO RELAX:
A 14 - Day Program

John D. Curtis, Ph.D.
and
Richard A. Detert

Coulee Press
La Crosse, Wisconsin

Learn To Relax:
A 14-Day Program

First Printing July 1983
Revised Edition January 1985
Second Printing July 1985
Third Printing October 1985

Coulee Press
P.O. Box 1744
La Crosse, Wisconsin 54602-1744, U.S.A.

Photographs by:
   John Arms/Corn's Photo Service, page 21
   Mark Beffart, page vi
   Roger A. Grant, pages 30-37
   Michael Hayman/Corn's Photo Service, pages iv & v
   Jerome Mooney, pages 8 & 9
   Florence Sharp, pages 86 & 93
   Vernon Sigl, page 2
Photographs pages 30-37 of:
   Judith S. McCaslin
   Phillip L. Esten
Graphic Design: Mary Abel
Copy Editor: Margaret S. Larson
Furniture: Scandianavian Design of La Crosse, Inc.

Library of Congress Cataloging in Publication Data

Curtis, John D.
   Learn To Relax.

   Bibliography: p.
   1. Relaxation. 2. Stress (Physiology) I. Detert,
Richard A. II. Title
RA785.C873   1983   613.7'9   83-7661
ISBN 0-9611456-1-7

TABLE OF CONTENTS

Learn to Relax: A 14-Day Program was written to fulfill a need that became apparent to us as we presented workshops, lectures and classes on stress management over the past ten years; namely, that most people do not have access to simple, understandable information on how to relax.

We discovered that people are concerned about their health and are willing to make a commitment to improve their health. However, finding accurate, understandable information and techniques that fit into one's schedule and lifestyle is often difficult. The lack of availability of classes, and the time and money to take them, also dampens the desire to improve one's health.

Therefore, we wrote this book in a "how to" format so you can learn to control stress, a major problem facing all of us today, by fitting relaxation into your daily routine. **Learn to Relax: A 14-Day Program** provides basic information and easy-to-follow relaxation techniques. These techniques will enable you to learn to relax with minimal time and monetary investment.

As with any health behavior change program, we recommend that you consult your physician before you begin this relaxation program.

This book is **not** designed to fulfill the need for a total stress management program. If you are interested in more detailed information regarding stress management, refer to the recommended readings and order form at the back of this book.

J.D.C. and R.A.D.

"To ward off disease or recover health, men as a rule find it easier to depend on the healers than to attempt the more difficult task of living wisely."

Rene' Dubos

The two-week relaxation program upon which you are about to embark is designed to fit into your schedule with relative ease. But be patient because it requires several days of practice before results can be observed. Follow the program as outlined and, within two weeks, you will be achieving deep relaxation without significantly changing your daily routine.

Work at the program diligently ... stay with it ... build it into your life on a permanent basis ... and begin "the more difficult task of living wisely."

RESULTS

The key to learning how to relax is to practice relaxation skills daily. Your body will relax by itself when it is ready.

Within one to five days of beginning the program, most people will notice the feelings of heaviness, sinking down, slowing down or a general feeling of warmth in the arms and/or the legs. These are the sensations of relaxation. Once any of these feelings is noticed, continued practice will bring about a deeper state of relaxation more quickly. Within approximately 14 days, you will be able to achieve an enjoyable state of deep muscular relaxation during most practice sessions.

The real benefits of relaxation, physical and psychological, usually appear after 4 to 10 weeks of regular, daily relaxation. However, some people will notice subtle physical and psychological changes within a week or two after beginning the program.

PART I

STRESS AND RELAXATION: OUR NEED FOR EACH

10

"I don't like tension but it tells me
something needs attending."

Hugh Prather

CHAPTER 1

Stress is killing you! Or is it? To understand the effects of stress, and the benefits of relaxation, one has to have a clear understanding of both terms.

Stress is defined as "a number of normal reactions for self-preservation." According to this definition, and contrary to popular belief, stress is not something to be avoided. Stress is a normal, desirable, beneficial part of our lives. Most people are more active, more invigorated, more creative, more productive, in general, more alive because of stress.

The stress response is meant to help us in life-threatening situations. It is a physical preparation of the body to deal with danger in order to increase our chances of survival. For example, when one of our ancestors encountered a dangerous animal, his body would respond almost instantly to prepare him for the physical fight with the animal or the physical flight from it. Hence, the stress response has been dubbed the "fight or flight" response.

When an individual perceives a threatening situation, and sets off the stress response, a variety of physiological changes occur:

- Increased sympathetic nervous system activity (the portion of the nervous system that prepares one for action)
- Increased body metabolism
  Increased heart rate
  Increased blood pressure
  Increased breathing rate
  Increased oxygen consumption
  Increased cardiac output
- Increased muscular tension
- Decreased blood clotting time (to help ensure survival if injured)
- Increased blood flow to the major muscle groups involved in the fight or flight (including the arms and legs)

These physiological changes, which occur almost instantaneously, prepare one for the physical exertion that may occur during the fight or flight. Each physical change, in one way or another, helps ensure survival. Thus, our ancestors who responded successfully to life-threatening stressors had a greater chance to live to reproductive age and pass on their genetic makeup to succeeding generations. As a result, modern man has a highly refined stress response.

THE PROBLEM WITH STRESS

The stress response is a life saver when used properly. However, when the stress response is set off too often and at improper times, it can have a detrimental effect on the body.

Stress most often becomes a problem in our lives when:

1 **The stress response is set off for inappropriate reasons.** This most often results when we perceive non-life-threatening situations to be stressful. We may perceive the car that doesn't start, rising taxes, job insecurity, or a breakdown in a relationship as being stressful. These are not life-threatening but if we perceive them as causing us some harm or frustration, the stress response and its accompanying physiological effects will take place in the body.

2 **Stress accumulates.** When the stress response is set off repeatedly over a short time period, the body doesn't have adequate time to adjust or return to normal between each stressor and the result is a buildup or an accumulation of stress. We refer to this buildup of stress as the "Staircase Effect" which is diagrammed in Figure 1-1.

STRESS-RELATED HEALTH PROBLEMS

There is evidence to suggest that too much stress and/or the inability to handle stress in our lives can lead to a variety of stress-related problems including:

Depression
Coronary heart disease
Peptic ulcer
Asthma
Diabetes
Lower back pain
Headaches
High blood pressure
Arthritis
Spastic bowel

Ulcerative colitis
Gout
Cancer
Skin rashes
Accidents
Multiple sclerosis
Mental health problems
Family violence
Child abuse
Suicide

FIGURE 1 - 1.   THE STAIRCASE EFFECT

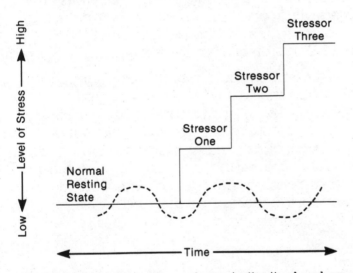

The body is designed to work most effectively when we fluctuate around the normal resting state which is illustrated with the dotted line. However, when we have inadequate time to return to our normal resting state after exposure to a stressor (stressor one), the physiological response of the next stressor (stressor two) will add to the remaining effects of the previous stress. This buildup or accumulation of stress is most often caused by setting off the stress response for inappropriate and non-life-threatening reasons.

In addition, many of today's most pressing health problems are related to the self-destructive habits of smoking, overeating, and substance abuse (including alcohol and other drugs). Many people turn to these maladaptive behaviors as a means of coping with stress.

Some researchers speculate an association exists between too much stress and the development of infectious diseases. Germs that cause many infectious diseases, such as colds, are often present without an individual getting sick or catching the cold. However, when a person has been under chronic or long-term stress, the body's defense mechanisms are worn down and, it is believed, the individual may be more susceptible to succumbing to the infectious disease.

Many people think of relaxation as engaging in some type of activity that is divergent from one's normal daily pattern. Activities such as reading, gardening, knitting, fishing, woodworking, and television are often considered relaxing. These types of activities are certainly constructive uses of leisure time and are extremely beneficial for our psychological well-being, but they are **not** "relaxation."

THE RELAXATION RESPONSE

Relaxation is "a physiological state that is, in general, the opposite of the stress state." Thus, relaxation involves developing a frame of mind that elicits a physiological state that is often referred to as the relaxation response. When a person achieves this "relaxed state," a variety of physiological changes occur including:
- Increased parasympathetic nervous system activity (this is the energy conservation branch of the nervous system)
- Decreased sympathetic nervous system activity
- Decreased body metabolism
  Decreased heart rate

Decreased blood pressure
Decreased breathing rate
Decreased oxygen consumption
Decreased cardiac output
• Decreased muscular tension
• Increased blood clotting time

These physiological changes can be brought about through relaxation training. When comparing these physiological reactions of the body to those that occur when a person is under stress, one can readily see that they are, in essence, the exact opposite. See Figure 2-1 for this comparison.

WHY RELAX?

There is increasing evidence that relaxation on a regular basis can be beneficial to one's health. A variety of professionals and researchers have found that relaxation, when practiced regularly,

1. is enjoyable;
2. can decrease symptoms of illness such as headache, nausea, rash, diarrhea;
3. can increase levels of physical energy;
4. can increase concentration;

FIGURE 2-1. Comparison of the Physiological Response During Stress and Relaxation

STRESS	RELAXATION
• Increased sympathetic nervous system activity	• Increased parasympathetic nervous system activity

• Increased body metabolism
    Increased heart rate
    Increased blood pressure
    Increased breathing rate
    Increased oxygen consumption
    Increased cardiac output
	• Decreased body metabolism
	    Decreased heart rate
	    Decreased blood pressure
	    Decreased breathing rate
	    Decreased oxygen consumption
	    Decreased cardiac output

• Increased muscular tension	• Decreased muscular tension
• Decreased blood clotting time	• Increased blood clotting time
• Increased blood flow to the major muscle groups involved in the fight-or-flight (including the arms and legs)	

5. can increase the ability to handle problems and increase overall efficiency;
6. can increase social satisfaction (e.g., in dealing with family, friends, and colleagues) and feelings of self-confidence;
7. is helpful in the treatment of insomnia;
8. can lower blood pressure;
9. can reduce severity of spastic esophagus;
10. can reduce severity of colitis;
11. can improve airway resistance for bronchial asthma;
12. can reduce headaches;
13. can lower emotional arousal, which seems to explain why some individuals do not overreact to stress.

In addition, researchers have found that people who report they relax on a regular basis:

1. are more psychologically stable;
2. are more physiologically stable;
3. are less anxious;
4. feel in greater control of their lives than people who do not practice regular relaxation;
5. achieve a faster return to a balance or normal state after reacting to stress.

PART II

"Relaxation is simple, but it is not easy. By this, I mean that relaxation techniques are very simple to do, but to motivate yourself to relax daily is not an easy task."

Jerry Braza, Ph.D.
University of Utah

It is important to have a clearly defined goal as you begin this program: **to achieve deep muscular relaxation in 14 days**. Set this goal firmly in your mind.

To accomplish it, we suggest the following ideas:

1. Make the goal a priority. Plan your daily schedule around the relaxation program. This requires that you set time aside to relax daily. The time commitment is a minor one compared to the benefits you will receive from daily relaxation.

2. Make up your mind that you will NEVER be too busy or too tired to relax. When you seem too busy or too tired, you need relaxation the most. Many people discover they derive the most benefit from relaxation at these times.

3. Concentrate on the excercises, but do so with a passive attitude. Turn your attention to the exercise. Feel, sense, and experience each exercise, but DON'T TRY TO RELAX. Just go through the exercise as best you can and your body will relax when it is ready.

4. Practice every day. To learn to relax within 14 days, you must relax on a daily basis. The time commitment will be minimal. The daily reminders along with the daily motivational techniques will be helpful in remembering to practice daily and will be useful in helping you evaluate your progress.

Good Luck and Keep Relaxing!

CHAPTER 3

When first beginning a relaxation program, remember:

1. This manual is designed for healthy individuals. If you have **any** health-related problems, whether physical or psychological, **check with your physician before starting this program.** This is absolutely necessary if you are using medication or are under any type of medical supervision. Have your physician or psychologist examine this book before you start.

2. You are always in control. There is not another person like you in the entire world. As a result, you may have to adapt certain exercises to meet your individual needs. If you have an unpleasant experience during an exercise, just flex, stretch, take a deep breath, and terminate the exercise. (See point 6 on how to terminate an excercise.)

3. Adjust for safety and comfort. Each person is unique and you may have to make some adjustments based on your individual situation. Things like removing contact lenses, loosening clothing, and selecting a position of comfort due to back problems may be helpful.

4. Sleep may occur during relaxation. Especially when first learning to relax, there is often a tendency to fall asleep. Adjust accordingly. If you set an alarm clock during the excercises, we suggest that you muffle the sound by placing it in a drawer, under a pillow or in an adjacent room. With practice, you will be able to achieve deep muscular relaxation for long periods without falling asleep.

5. Practice in a quiet environment. This will reduce distractions and enhance your opportunity to achieve deep relaxation. It is much easier to concentrate on a relaxation exercise when there is little or no noise to interfere with relaxation. However, once relaxation is mastered, noise and other distractions will not bother you as much, if at all. You may even discover you can use noise to aid you in your relaxation efforts. This will increase the number of places where you can relax.

6. Ending a relaxation exercise is similar to awakening from sleep. To terminate an exercise simply take a deep breath as you flex, stretch, and open your eyes.

7. Record daily progress. Keep track of your relaxation on the charts provided. These charts will help you incorporate relaxation into your daily schedule and allow you to recognize improvements in your ability to relax.

SELECTING A POSITION

When preparing to relax, it is important to select a body position that will not hinder relaxation. The position selected should not cause muscular tension, inhibit circulation, invite cramps or provoke unnecessary movement or effects. The position should enhance a person's ability to "let go" and relax. The following suggestions should help you select a position for your relaxation program.

1. The position selected **must meet your needs.** Everyone is different, and no one position or combination of positions will serve everyone. Select and/or adapt a position to meet your needs, preferences and physical requirements.

2. The position should be comfortable and have a minimum of muscular tension. To decrease the muscular tension required to maintain the body in place, the position should provide maximum support for as many body parts as possible.

3. The body should be well aligned, that is, the right side of the body should be in the same position as the left side. This allows for greater stability when in a deeply relaxed state.

4. The arms and legs should be supported. This will help ensure a minimum amount of muscular tension.

5. The arms and hands, and the legs and feet, should not be crossed or touching. When body parts cross or touch, sweating, impaired circulation, limbs "falling asleep," and cramping often occur. All of these interfere with relaxation.

6. It is easiest to learn the skills in positions that provide maximum support for the body, i.e., back-lying, easy chair and recliner positions. After the skills have been learned, the exercises can be done just as effectively in minimum support positions.

7. After mastering relaxation, practice in positions that provide minimum support. With practice, you can relax just as deeply in minimum support positions, thus increasing the number of settings in which you can relax (e.g., airplanes, bus terminals, sitting on a bench or chair, riding in a car).

Maximum Support Positions

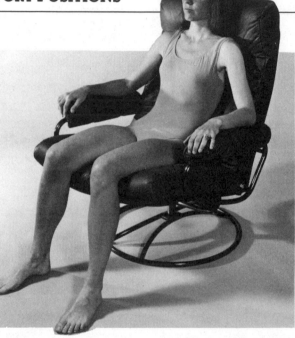

Easy Chair Position

This position requires a high-back chair. To assume the position, sit in the chair, lean back, and allow the chair to support the head, back, buttocks, and thighs. Your arms should rest on the arms of the chair or on your lap and your feet and legs should be spread comfortably with the feet flat on the floor. Adjust the position so that you are comfortable. This is a position of maximum support and can be used effectively when first learning to relax.

BACK LYING POSITION

Lay in a supine position with the arms resting comfortably at your sides with the elbows in a slightly flexed position. The legs should be comfortably spread apart. Many people prefer to use a pillow under the head, but only a very small one should be used so tension is not created in the head and neck region. It is best to use a small pillow or towel rolled up under the neck so that the chin is elevated.

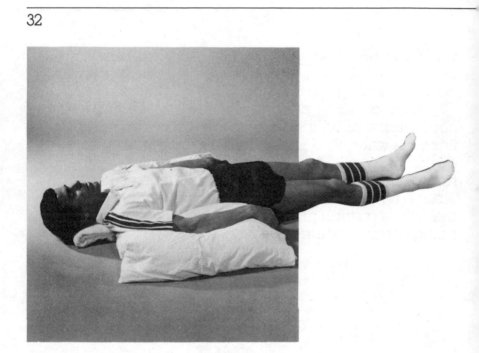

(Variations Of Back Lying Position)

Arm And Shoulder Support

Pillows or blankets are used under the arms and/or shoulders to eliminate tension in the chest and shoulder region. Arm and shoulder support is especially helpful when lying on a hard surface such as a floor.

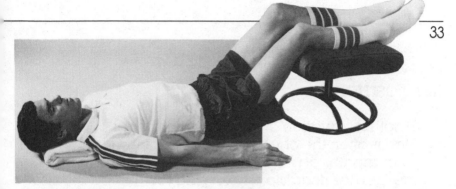

KNEE SUPPORT

Individuals with back problems may have to elevate the knees to reduce low back pain or tightness. The elevation of the knees flattens the lower back and reduces the tension. Pillows or blankets can be used as shown below. A chair can also be used as shown above. In either case, support must exist under the knees so that the knees are bent. The elevation must be of an appropriate height so that you are comfortable.

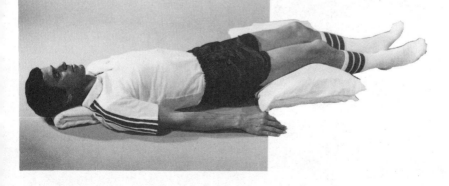

SIDE POSITION

Another variation of the back lying position. This position is often the choice of pregnant women during the later months of pregnancy. Other individuals that cannot get comfortable when lying on their backs also use this variation.

RECLINER POSITION

This is similar to the easy chair position. The use of a reclining chair offers many adjustable positions, all of which offer excellent support and are helpful when learning to relax. For best results, be sure the recliner is the proper size for your body.

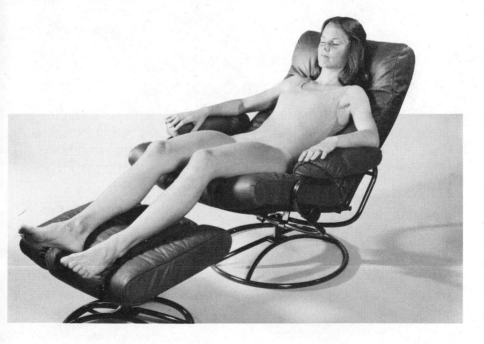

FORWARD LEANING SITTING POSITION

This position requires active use of various muscles to maintain it. Thus, tension exists because the body is not entirely supported by the chair. However, the position can be used in a variety of places since it does not require back support.

To assume this position, sit down on a chair, bench, toilet seat or some other place where support for the buttocks is provided. The arms and hands should be supported by the legs, and the feet should be comfortably spread apart and flat on the ground. The head can either hang forward or, if that is not comfortable, lean back until it is balanced upright with as little tension as possible.

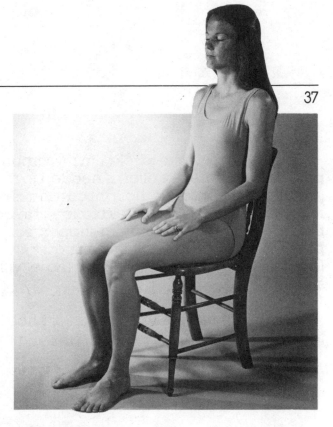

UPRIGHT SITTING POSITION

To assume the upright sitting position, some type of back support is needed in addition to support for the buttocks. Support is provided for the lower back and the buttocks by the chair and for the feet by the floor. The arms and the hands should rest on the upper legs or on the arms of the chair. The feet should be flat on the floor and comfortably spread apart. The head can hang forward or be held upright, whichever is more comfortable.

It is easiest to learn to relax in maximum support positions because less effort is needed to maintain the position and conscious thought can focus on the relaxation itself. Once the relaxation can be done easily, begin to practice in minimum support positions. With practice, you can learn to relax as quickly and as deeply in minimal support positions as in those with maximum support.

Above all, remember to adjust or choose a position that works for you.

CHAPTER 4

RELAXATION TECHNIQUES

It is time to begin the relaxation program!

1. The techniques are presented in sequence. Learn each technique in the order presented.

2. To enhance the learning effect, practice each technique according to the schedules listed in the daily reminders that begin on page 70.

3. To learn the exercises, read each one through several times before you attempt to perform it. You should become familiar with the exercise but you should NOT try to memorize it.

Words that are hyphenated letter-by-letter (e.g., s-i-n-k-i-n-g d-o-w-n) should be repeated slowly in your mind in time with the exhalation phase of your breathing cycle.

Periods (...) indicate a pause. The length of the pause is determined by the number of periods used. The more periods, the longer the pause (i.e., ... is twice as long as ....).

4. Understand the breathing rhythms. Each exercise is based on using the breathing rhythms for relaxation.

5. If using the **Learn to Relax: A 14-Day Program** cassette tape that is designed to accompany this book, read the instructions that come with the tape.

THE BREATHING RHYTHM

To understand the relaxation techniques, an understanding of the breathing cycle and its use in relaxation is needed. The breathing cycle has two distinct phases — the inhalation phase and the exhalation phase.

INHALATION PHASE: The inhalation phase of the breathing cycle is the invigoration or tension-producing phase. When performing relaxation skills, obviously you do not want to produce tension. However, the inhalation portion of the breathing cycle is important in reversing the relaxed state and is used to come out of the relaxed state. When ready to terminate an exercise, a deep breath or two should be taken. This deep inhalation will create tension and help bring you back to your normal level of alertness. Somewhat like a yawn, deep inhalation in usually combined with the flexing and stretching of muscles much like one does when awakening from a state of sleep.

EXHALATION PHASE: The exhalation phase of the breathing cycle is the relaxation phase. If attention is focused on the exhalation phase, a feeling of **sinking down, slowing down, heaviness,** and in general a feeling of **relaxation** is felt. These sensations (sinking down, slowing down, heaviness, and general relaxation), when felt during the exhalation phase of the breathing cycle, will carry you into a state of relaxation.

USING THE BREATHING RHYTHMS TO RELAX

The basic techniques in this book all use the exhalation phase of the breathing cycle to achieve a feeling of relaxation. To perform each of these techniques, you must remember and follow four basic criteria.

1. Breathe normally. Observe the breathing cycle passively. In other words, let your body breathe by itself and quietly observe yourself breathe just as if you were a bystander.

2. Disregard the inhalations. **Do not** think about the inhalations at all. Just permit your body to inhale by itself without any conscious thought on your part.

3. Focus your attention on the exhalation phase of the breathing cycle. Concentrate and think about the exhalations.

4. Feel and experience key sensations as you exhale. The sensations you may notice are sinking down, slowing down, heaviness, and an overall letting go or feeling of relaxation. **The key to the breathing rhythms is to feel the sensations as you exhale - and only as you exhale. To enhance the relaxation effect, you must synchronize the key feelings with the exhalation phase.**

THE EXHALATION EXERCISE

DESCRIPTION

The exhalation exercise will establish the exhalation phase of your breathing cycle as the cue for relaxation to occur within your body. It will establish the ground rules for the three remaining exercises. As you perform this exercise remember to (1) breathe normally; (2) disregard the inhalations; (3) focus your attention on the exhalation phase of the breathing cycle; and (4) feel, sense and experience the key sensations as you exhale.

DIRECTIONS

Assume a comfortable relaxation position with as much support as possible. Do not cross the arms or legs. During this exercise, be sure to maintain a passive attitude and to allow relaxation to occur.

When ready, allow yourself to close your eyes and, for the first several (e.g., two to five) breathing cycles, quietly observe the air as it enters and leaves your nose . . . .

Now, for the next several breaths, focus only on the exhalation phase of the breathing cycle, notice the warmth of the air as it leaves your nose and r-e-l-a-x as

you exhale .... and r-e-l-a-x as you exhale ....
and allow yourself to l-e-t g-o as you continue to focus on
your exhalations .... and r-e-l-a-x as you
exhale .... and r-e-l-a-x as you exhale ....
....

N ow, as you exhale, feel or sense the body
s-i-n-k-i-n-g d-o-w-n into the supporting environment ....
....

N otice the body sinking d-o-w-n .... and d-o-w-n,
more and more with each exhalation ....
....

A t this time, as you exhale, feel the body s-l-o-w-i-n-g
d-o-w-n .... You
may notice the breathing rhythm slowing down, or
possibly the heart beat slowing down ...., or possibly
just an overall sense of patience .... Each time you
notice any of these sensations, allow the body to let go
and relax more and more .... letting go, sinking
down, and r-e-l-a-x-i-n-g ....

N ow, remain in the relaxed state for several
moments .... and, when ready to end the

relaxation, take a deep breath as you flex, stretch, and open your eyes.

DAILY REMINDER

Turn to page 70 for your practice goals and recording log for exercise one. Do not move on to exercise two until day three.

EXERCISE TWO

The second phase of the deep relaxation program incorporates the exhalation exercise with relaxation of specific body parts. This is done in a sequential manner throughout the body, thus the name sequential relaxation.

DESCRIPTION
Sequential relaxation will use the exhalation phase of the breathing rhythm to allow specific body parts to relax. When the sensation of relaxation develops in a body part, attention will be moved to another body part until that one is relaxed. This is continued until total body relaxation is achieved. To perform this exercise, you should follow the criteria listed below:

1. Focus your attention on a specific body part. Although it is not essential, for the sake of simplicity we recommend that you use the following sequence:
foot; lower leg (calf region); upper leg (thigh); buttocks and hips; trunk (including shoulders); arms and hands.

2. As you exhale, feel the sensations of relaxation occur in the body part on which you are focusing. The sensations to expect are sinking down, slowing down, heaviness, and general relaxation.

3. Once the sensation of relaxation is identified in the

body part you are focusing on, or after you have spent two to four breathing cycles on the body part (regardless of whether you have identified the relaxed sensations or not), move your focus of attention to the corresponding body part if there is one (e.g., from right foot to left foot, right lower leg to left lower leg) or to the next body part in sequence (e.g., foot to lower leg, or lower leg to upper leg).

4. Move through the body in sequence until the major body parts have been covered and relaxation has occurred.

5. Remain in the relaxed state until you are ready to terminate the exercise and come back to an alert state. Then, take a deep breath as you flex, stretch, and open your eyes.

DIRECTIONS

Assume a comfortable position and, when ready, allow you eyes to close. For several breathing cycles, quietly and passively listen to yourself breathe ....
. . .

And now, turn your attention to just the exhalation phase of your breathing cycle .... and r-e-l-a-x as you exhale .... exhale and r-e-l-a-x .... simply permit yourself to l-e-t go .... and r-e-l-a-x more and more with each exhalation ....

Now, focus on your right foot and ankle, and as you exhale notice the tension flow out of that foot and ankle .. .. notice that foot and ankle become slightly heavy and more and more r-e-l-a-x-e-d .... As you notice this, allow the foot and ankle to s-i-n-k d-o-w-n and become totally supported by the floor .... As you exhale, notice a s-i-n-k-i-n-g d-o-w-n of the foot into the supporting environment ....

And now, ... focus your attention on the left foot and ankle .... and allow it to let go and r-e-l-a-x with your exhalations .... allow that foot and ankle to become slightly h-e-a-v-y, ... and more and more relaxed with each exhalation ....

At this time, move your attention to your right lower leg (the calf region) .... As you focus on this area, allow the muscles to r-e-l-a-x .... to l-e-t g-o as you

exhale .... simply allow the tensions to flow
out of the lower leg as you e-x-h-a-l-e .... and r-e-
l-a-x ....

Move your attention to the left lower leg and, with
each exhalation, feel the muscles of the left lower leg
s-i-n-k-i-n-g d-o-w-n .... and becoming slightly h-e-a-v-y
....

And now, move your attention to the right thigh .....
and feel that part of the body r-e-l-a-x as you exhale ....
.... and r-e-l-a-x as you exhale ....

And now, focus your attention on the left thigh. Feel
and experience a l-e-t-t-i-n-g g-o with each exhalation.

Focus now on both legs and notice a comfortable
heaviness develop with each exhalation as you
experience the gentle pull of gravity on the legs ....
....

And now, let the relaxation in your legs flow into the
buttocks and hips .... As you exhale, allow the
muscles to r-e-l-a-x and feel the buttocks s-i-n-k-i-n-g
d-o-w-n into the supporting environment as you exhale ...

. . . .

Now, let this relaxation flow into the trunk area as you exhale and r-e-l-a-x . . . . Feel the trunk sinking down and becoming c-o-m-f-o-r-t-a-b-l-y h-e-a-v-y with each exhalation . . . .

Focus your attention on the right arm and hand and, as you exhale, allow the relaxation to flow into the right arm and hand. Feel it s-i-n-k-i-n-g d-o-w-n and becoming c-o-m-f-o-r-t-a-b-l-y h-e-a-v-y as you feel the gentle pull of gravity exert itself on the right arm . . . .

Now, allow relaxation to move into the left arm . . . . Feel the left arm becoming c-o-m-f-o-r-t-a-b-l-y h-e-a-v-y . . . . more and more r-e-l-a-x-e-d with each exhalation . . . .

Now, allow this relaxation to flow into the entire body with each exhalation. Feel, sense and experience a comfortable heaviness . . . . or a general slowing down of the body . . . . Allow the body now to establish its own pace . . . . and r-e-l-a-x as you exhale . . . . and r-e-l-a-x as you exhale . . . .

Allow this relaxation to occur until you are ready to terminate the exercise. Then take a deep breath as you flex, stretch, and open your eyes.

DAILY REMINDER

Turn to page 72 for your practice goals and recording log for exercise two. Do exercises one and two as listed in your daily goals for days three through six. Do not move on to exercise three until day seven.

Exercise Three

The Sensory Awareness Exercise

52

DESCRIPTION

The sensory awareness exercise is designed to help you become more consciously aware of sensory perceptions and sensations that exist within your body. As you tune into and develop a more heightened awareness of your body and permit it to set its own pace, a feeling of calmness, slowing down, and relaxation will occur.

DIRECTIONS

Whenever you are ready, assume a comfortable, relaxing position, allow your eyes to close, and for several breathing cycles, focus on your exhalations, listening to yourself breathe, feeling the warmth of the air as it leaves your nose . . . .

As you continue to focus on your exhalations, feel the gentle pull of gravity as it exerts itself on your body . . . .

Feel and sense your body s·i·n·k·i·n·g d·o·w·n . . . . s·l·o·w·i·n·g d·o·w·n . . . . and r·e·l·a·x·i·n·g as you exhale.

Pay attention to everything that is happening within your body. When you identify something happening, such as an itch on the hand, a twitching of the eyelid, or a churning of the stomach (see Figure 4-1 for examples of other sensations to search for), mentally acknowledge that occurrence, focus on your exhalations, and continue to scan the body for other sensations.

Each time you identify something, simply acknowledge that sensation and then move your attention to other body parts, searching yet for more sensations.

After a few moments, you will notice a general quieting of the body, and a calm state will occur. Simply permit the body to set its own pace. After you begin to feel relaxed, go back to the breathing cycles and, as you exhale, allow your body to become more and more relaxed, feeling a s-i-n-k-i-n-g d-o-w-n....a s-l-o-w-i-n-g d-o-w-n....a l-e-t-t-i-n-g g-o............................

Remain in this relaxed state until you are ready to terminate the exercise. At that time, you will simply flex, stretch, inhale and open your eyes.

FIGURE 4-1.   SENSATIONS TO SEARCH FOR

Coolness	Twitching
Warmth	Pressure
Hardness	Eyes Fluttering
Expansion (Chest)	An Itch
Tightening	Stillness
Heaviness	Movement
Swallowing	Churning of Stomach

DAILY REMINDER:
Turn to page 76 for your practice goals and recording log for exercise three. Add this exercise to one and two as listed in your daily goals for days seven through ten. Do not move on to exercise four until day ten.

Exercise four is an abbreviated form of exercise one. It is designed to bring you to a deeply relaxed state in a shorter period of time than with the three previous exercises. It will work most effectively if you have been able to relax with the previous exercises. If you have had any difficulty, you may find it helpful to spend several additional days on exercises one, two and three before beginning this one. The Brief Exhalation Exercise will illustrate how simply and quickly deep relaxation can be instilled within the body.

DESCRIPTION

Once the sensations of sinking down, slowing down, heaviness, and general relaxation can be felt in specific body parts, an abbreviated form of exercise one is used. Exercise four involves the same general concepts as exercise one:

Breathe normally;

Disregard the inhalations;

Focus your attention on the exhalations;

Feel the sinking down, slowing down, heaviness, and general relaxation **only** during the exhalations.

DIRECTIONS

Assume a comfortable position in which the body is well supported.... and, when you are ready, focus on your exhalations and allow your eyes to close..............
...

For the next several breathing cycles, passively listen to, or observe, yourself breathe........

Listen to the air as it moves into and out of your nose and feel the warmth of the air on the exhalation...........
....

And now, focus your attention only on the exhalation phase of your breathing......and r-e-l-a-x as you exhale......and r-e-l-a-x as you exhale,......simply permit yourself to l-e-t g-o and r-e-l-a-x as you exhale......
....

And now, as you continue to focus on your exhalation,......feel the body s-i-n-k-i-n-g d-o-w-n into the chair, the bed, or the floor......letting go......sinking down and letting go each and every time you exhale....
....

Continue to experience this letting go until you are ready to return to the normal, alert state. At that time, take a deep breath as you flex, stretch, and open your eyes.

DAILY REMINDER

Turn to page 80 for your practice goals and recording log for exercise four. Add exercise four to the previous three as listed in your daily goals for days eleven through fourteen.

CHAPTER 5

QUESTIONS AND ANSWERS

JUST EXACTLY WHAT IS RELAXATION?
Relaxation is a systematic means of bringing about physiological changes in the body that are opposite from the stress response. Relaxation exercises serve as a "systematic means" to relax both the mind and the body. You are able to "cruise in neutral" - a state where the body and mind are restored from the wear and tear of living.

WHY SHOULD A PERSON TAKE TIME TO RELAX?
Studies have shown that people who relax regularly are less anxious, psychologically and physiologically more stable, and have greater control over their lives. People have also reported sleeping better, feeling less fatigued at the end of the day, being more productive at work, and getting along better with others. Studies have also demonstrated beneficial results in controlling many of the stress-related diseases.

HOW MUCH TIME DOES ONE HAVE TO SPEND RELAXING TO ACHIEVE BENEFITS?
In our hectic, fast-paced society, any time spent allowing the mind and body to recoup is beneficial. For maximum benefits, we recommend two ten-minute sessions or one twenty-minute session every day. If you

notice increased tension during the day, periodic three-
to five-minute sessions can also be extremely helpful.

WHEN IS THE BEST TIME TO RELAX?
The best time to relax is when you perceive a need
to slow down or to get out from under the pressure
cooker. Some individuals prefer to relax in the early
morning; others mid-morning; still others late in the
afternoon. Each person will need to decide when and
how relaxation best can be incorporated into a daily
schedule without causing stress. If there is one general
rule of when not to relax, it is immediately after eating.
Otherwise, it's your choice.

DO I NEED SOMEONE OR SOMETHING TO GUIDE ME?
Although a trained relaxation technician or a
relaxation tape can be beneficial when learning to
relax, they are not necessary. Actually, each person
allows relaxation to occur; it does not happen because
of the technician or tape. Learn to listen to and guide
yourself through relaxation exercises. In this way, you
can relax whenever and wherever you are—not only if
there is a tape recorder available.

ARE RELAXATION AND SLEEP THE SAME?

NO! Both sleep and relaxation are altered states of consciousness but at different levels. Sleep can be physically restless and a time for the mind to work out the stresses of life. During deep relaxation, there is little or no anxiety. Actually, deep relaxation is even more restful than sleep. However, relaxation is not a substitute for sleep, nor is sleep a substitute for relaxation. The body and mind require both.

CAN RELAXATION BE HARMFUL?

In a general sense, NO! It is no more harmful than praying for the same period of time. Anyone taking medication, especially prescribed by a physician, should check with a physician before embarking on a relaxation program. Occasionally, the mixture of chemicals and deep relaxation may be counterproductive to health. The best advice here is to use your best judgment and, if there is any question whatever, call your health-care provider.

WHAT CAN I DO ABOUT "DISTRACTING THOUGHTS" WHILE I'M TRYING TO RELAX?

The first thing to recognize is that there will be times when your mind will wander while you are trying to relax, especially when you are under a great deal of stress and/or time deadlines. Should you try to force these thoughts away or become irritated by them, tension will be created and the ability to relax lessened. When these thoughts occur, remain passive, acknowledge them, and let them serve as a cue for you to return first to your exhalations and then continue the relaxation exercise. With practice you will soon discover that the distracting thoughts will become fewer and you will be able to relax without the mind wandering.

WILL RELAXING EVERY DAY LEAD TO LAZINESS?
The core of the question seems to be "will taking time to relax make me less productive?" NO! Several studies indicate that people who take five or ten minutes to relax during coffee breaks or other planned times during the day are actually more productive than those who don't. Taking time to allow the body to slow down, reduce fatigue, and energize allows for better pacing, increased stamina, and increased work efficiency.

CHAPTER 6

PUTTING THE PROGRAM INTO ACTION

MOTIVATIONAL TOOLS

Relaxation, like many health behaviors, is simple—but it's not easy. Relaxation techniques are simple to learn, but they are not easy to put into practice on a daily basis. The most difficult part of learning how to relax is to **remember** to relax each day or, if you remember, to find the time to build it into your daily routine. To learn to relax often means changing your established habits.

Habits, both desirable and undesirable, are difficult to change. Once a habit is developed, it requires a conscious effort to alter it. To be successful at "snapping the stress cycle," managing stress and incorporating regular relaxation into our daily schedule, old habits need to be changed or substituted with new ones. We have found the following basic techniques to be useful in developing the positive habit of regular relaxation.

SCHEDULE RELAXATION

Make relaxation a priority. Place it on top of your daily "to do list" and build it into your schedule. Otherwise, it probably won't get done. And remember, schedule relaxation first; then build the rest of your daily schedule around it. Avoid doing it the opposite way.

REMINDER CARDS

Reminder cards can be used in several ways. First, make up some colorful and eye-catching three-by-five cards with sayings such as "Relax," "Take a vacation every day," "Take a little bit of time every day to do yourself a favor ... relax," "Take five," "R", etc. Place these cards where you will see them regularly, e.g., taped to a mirror, on your desk, in a locker, in your lunch bag, on top of your daily "to do list," in a dresser drawer, in your wallet or purse, or on your calendar. Whenever you see the card, mentally remind yourself to relax, take a break, and perform a relaxation exercise.

Another effective means of using reminder cards is to record your relaxation exercises on the back of them and keep a tally of how often and how long you do them. At the end of the day, you can transfer the information to your daily reminder. Remember, as long as you are aware of relaxation and think of it regularly, you can develop a regular habit of relaxation. Awareness is the key.

SUBSTITUTION REMINDER

Select several objects that are meaningful to you and that you encounter or think of daily. Whenever you view these objects, e.g., a photograph or a music box, use them as a reminder to think of relaxation and perform a relaxation exercise. One student reported using a key that hung on a chain in her room. Whenever she sat down, she saw it hanging on the wall and used this as her "key to success" and practiced her relaxation skills.

LINK RELAXATION WITH AN ESTABLISHED HABIT
Use a habit already established in your life as the link to relaxation. If you exercise regularly, you may want to tie in your relaxation with your exercise. Many people report that one of the easiest times to relax is following exercise, so use a relaxation technique after your warm-down. Some people find that doing relaxation exercises prior to leaving work is beneficial because it provides a natural break between work and the relaxed after-hours environment. Others relax upon waking up each morning, while waiting for an appointment, prior to going to sleep at night, or before a meal. The key is to link relaxation practice with a firmly established habit that is done on a regular basis.

RELATE IT TO STRESS OR QUIETNESS
Whenever you become aware of undesired stress, such as a tense neck, relax; or whenever you find yourself in a quiet environment or have "waiting time"

perform relaxation skills.

TELEVISION

As odd as it may seem, television may be a key to relaxation for some. Several mothers reported doing relaxation skills during T.V. shows. As an example, one mother reported that her young children were allowed to watch only two shows a day: "Sesame Street" in the morning and "Mash" in the evening. While the youngsters were tuned into TV, mom was tuned into her breathing rhythms and relaxing.

USING SCENERY AS A CUE

"For example, one of my favorite techniques is to use scenery as a reminder. Towering bluffs, 600 feet high, border our city. The bluffs are not only beautiful but also relaxing because they remind one of nature - if one only takes the time to 'see' the bluffs daily. Whenever I view the bluffs, they are a mental reminder to myself to relax, do a body search for tensions, check my pace to see if I am hurried and, if so, to slow my pace down. I see the bluffs many times a day and, thus, get regular reminders to tune inward, read the signals of my body, and plan a time for relaxation exercise if necessary." J.D.C.

RESULTS THEMSELVES MAY BE MOTIVATIONAL

Many people find that the results they obtain from regular practice are motivational in themselves. A reduction in headaches (number or severity), sleeping sounder, feeling less hurried, less tense and more composed are all positive reinforcers to regular periods of relaxation. Many report regular practice has increased concentration in work, study, and sports while others report a drop in their blood pressure. These improvements, plus many others, may be motivation enough to remind you of regular practice.

DAILY REMINDER

Keeping track of your daily periods of relaxation has been one of the most successful motivational tools we have found. Keeping a daily log, in which you write down each practice session, serves as a reminder throughout the day to remember to relax.

These motivational techniques are not necessarily the best answers to meet your needs. We share these examples from which you can build your own because the most successful motivational techniques are developed by the individual employing them. We encourage you to find the best techniques because we believe that failure to develop a plan with motivational and reinforcing tools will result in less than hoped for results from your relaxation program.

DAILY REMINDER

This is your 14-day progress report. Read the guidelines below:

1. Record your progress each day. When **no** exercises were performed, enter a **zero**.

2. Practice each and every day, weekends included! Make daily relaxation a **habit**.

3. Think of the Daily Reminder as a motivational and reinforcement tool. Be proud of your day-to-day progress as you accomplish your daily goal.

4. The daily goal listed is the **minimum** number of minutes needed for that day. You are encouraged to practice more than the minimum and thus accumulate more minutes per day than the number suggested.

5. You will receive credit for **each minute** of **"relaxation practice"** done **each day** whether you feel relaxed or not. Example: If you practiced two times per day, three minutes the first time and two minutes the second time, you would record five minutes (three plus two). See sample of Daily Reminder on the opposite page.

6. Practice session numbers printed in **bold**, indicate the minimum number of practice sessions for that day. Additional practice sessions are listed so that you may practice more than the minimum. (In the example below two practice sessions are required.)

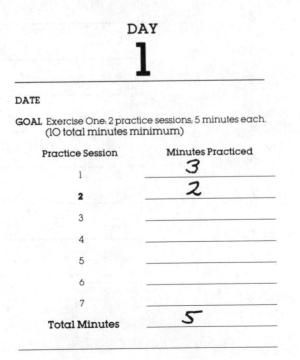

DAY
1

DATE

GOAL Exercise One: 2 practice sessions: 5 minutes each. (10 total minutes minimum)

Practice Session	Minutes Practiced
1	3
2	2
3	
4	
5	
6	
7	
Total Minutes	5

DAY
1

DATE

GOAL Exercise One: 2 practice sessions; 5 minutes each.
(10 total minutes minimum)

Practice Session	Minutes Practiced
1	
2	
3	
4	
5	
6	
7	
Total Minutes	

DAY
2

DATE

GOAL Exercise One: 2 practice sessions; 5 minutes each.
(10 total minutes minimum)

Practice Session	Minutes Practiced
1	_____
2	_____
3	_____
4	_____
5	_____
6	_____
7	_____
Total Minutes	_____

DAY
3

DATE

GOAL Exercise One: 1 session; 4 minutes total.
Exercise Two: 1 session; 6 minutes total.
(10 total minutes minimum)

Practice Session	Minutes Practiced
1	
2	
3	
4	
5	
6	
7	
Total Minutes	

DAY
4

DATE

GOAL Exercise One: 1 session; 4 minutes total.
Exercise Two: 2 sessions; 4 minutes each.
(12 total minutes minimum)

Practice Session	Minutes Practiced
1	_____
2	_____
3	_____
4	_____
5	_____
6	_____
7	_____
Total Minutes	_____

DAY
5

DATE

GOAL Exercise One: 1 session; 5 minutes total.
Exercise Two: 2 sessions; 5 minutes each.
(15 total minutes minimum)

Practice Session	Minutes Practiced
1	_____
2	_____
3	_____
4	_____
5	_____
6	_____
7	_____
Total Minutes	_____

74

DAY
6

DATE

GOAL Exercise One: 1 session; 5 minutes total.
Exercise Two: 2 sessions; 5 minutes each.
(15 total minutes minimum)

Practice Session	Minutes Practiced
1	_____
2	_____
3	_____
4	_____
5	_____
6	_____
7	_____
Total Minutes	_____

DAY
7

DATE

GOAL Exercise One: 1 session; 4 minutes total.
Exercise Two: 1 session; 4 minutes total.
Exercise Three: 2 sessions; 4 minutes each.
(16 total minutes minimum)

Practice Session	Minutes Practiced
1	
2	
3	
4	
5	
6	
7	
Total Minutes	

DAY

8

DATE

GOAL Exercise One: 1 session; 4 minutes total.
Exercise Two: 1 session; 4 minutes total.
Exercise Three: 2 sessions; 4 minutes each.
(16 total minutes minimum)

Practice Session	Minutes Practiced
1	_____
2	_____
3	_____
4	_____
5	_____
6	_____
7	_____
Total Minutes	_____

DAY
9

DATE

GOAL Exercise One: 1 session; 3 minutes total.
Exercise Two: 1 session; 4 minutes total.
Exercise Three: 2 sessions; 5 minutes each.
(17 total minutes minimum)

Practice Session	Minutes Practiced
1	
2	
3	
4	
5	
6	
7	
Total Minutes	

DAY
10

DATE

GOAL Exercise One or Two: 2 sessions; 5 minutes each.
Exercise Three: 2 sessions; 4 minutes each.
(18 total minutes minimum)

Practice Session	Minutes Practiced
1	_____
2	_____
3	_____
4	_____
5	_____
6	_____
7	_____
Total Minutes	_____

DAY
11

DATE

GOAL Exercise One or Two: 1 session; 5 minutes.
Exercise Three: 1 session; 5 minutes.
Exercise Four: 2 sessions; 4 minutes each.
(18 total minutes minimum)

Practice Session	Minutes Practiced
1	
2	
3	
4	
5	
6	
7	
Total Minutes	

DAY
12

DATE

GOAL Exercise One, Two, or Three: 1 session; 6 minutes.
Exercise Four: 2 sessions; 5 minutes each.
(16 total minutes minimum)

Practice Session	Minutes Practiced
1	_____
2	_____
3	_____
4	_____
5	_____
6	_____
7	_____
Total Minutes	_____

DAY
13

DATE

GOAL Exercise One Or Two: 1 session; 6 minutes.
Exercise Three: 1 session; 6 minutes.
Exercise Four: 1 session; 8 minutes.
(20 total minutes minimum)

Practice Session	Minutes Practiced
1	_____
2	_____
3	_____
4	_____
5	_____
6	_____
7	_____
Total Minutes	_____

DAY
14

DATE

GOAL Any sequence which totals 18 minutes
or more on a daily basis.

Practice Session	Minutes Practiced
1	_____
2	_____
3	_____
4	_____
5	_____
6	_____
7	_____
Total Minutes	_____

DAY

DATE

GOAL Any sequence which totals 18 minutes
or more on a daily basis.

Practice Session	Minutes Practiced
1	_____
2	_____
3	_____
4	_____
5	_____
6	_____
7	_____
Total Minutes	_____

DAY

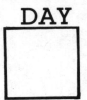

DATE

GOAL Any sequence which totals 18 minutes
or more on a daily basis.

Practice Session	Minutes Practiced
1	_____
2	_____
3	_____
4	_____
5	_____
6	_____
7	_____
Total Minutes	_____

PART III

CHAPTER 7

INSTANT RELAXATION

We use the term **Instant Relaxation** to represent a variety of relaxation techniques with perceptible results within a five to forty-five second period. Relaxation techniques that fall under this classification are generally short and easy to do. Since these **Instant Relaxation (IR)** techniques are based upon the skills perfected in the **Learn to Relax 14 - Day Basic Program**, we suggest that you complete the basic program before you try the **IR** techniques. Although this is not a requirement for success, we have found that the techniques are learned most effectively this way.

ADVANTAGES OF INSTANT RELAXATION

Although **IR** techniques do not take the place of deep muscle relaxation, they do offer many advantages and thus complement the basic **Learn to Relax** skills. Listed below are some of the advantages of **Instant Relaxation:**

1. **IR** techniques can be done anywhere. You don't need to close your eyes, have quiet surroundings, or mentally withdraw from the environment.

2. IR techniques are quick and easy to do. They can thus be done throughout the day—whenever you have five to ten seconds or more.

3. IR techniques complement basic relaxation techniques by raising your consciousness of tension levels throughout the body. Once you are aware of tensions, **Instant Relaxation** can be used to lower these levels (see No. 4 below).

4. When practiced regularly, the **IR** techniques can help reduce unwanted muscle tension and fatigue.

5. The **IR** techniques are an extension of the basic program techniques. For instance, each technique uses the exhalation phase of the breathing rhythm as your cue for the body to relax.

The **IR** techniques work most effectively when done throughout the day (ten or more times per day). Therefore, they should be linked with an established occurrence that recurs throughout the day to help serve as a reminder to do the techinques. For example, you may use the telephone or your watch as your cue. Each time the phone rings or you look at the time, use that behavior as a reminder to do an **IR** technique to reduce unwanted muscle tension.

Caution: When doing the **IR** techniques do not take more than two or three deep breaths. Repeated deep breathing in some people can lead to hyperventilation and/or light-headedness.

The R And R Technique (Relax And Respond)

The R and R is a two-breath tension-control technique that can be done in five to fifteen seconds. The first exhalation is the relaxation portion while the second exhalation is the responding phase.

The relaxation breath: Take a deep breath and, as you exhale, allow the body to relax, sink down and become heavy.

The respond breath: Take in a second breath and, as you exhale, respond (i.e., return to your previous activity; for example, answer the telephone).

If time permits, you may want to repeat the first breath several times before the respond breath. If you do, be sure to use a normal breath on successive inhalations.

The Deep Breath Technique

The Deep Breath is a one-breath technique that can be repeated if desired. Each successive breath should be a normal breath and not a deep breath.

Take in a deep breath and hold it for a count of five. As you exhale, feel the body sinking down and becoming heavy and relaxed.

THE STRETCH TECHNIQUE

This technique uses a stretch to create muscle tension and the exhalation phase to relax the body.

Take in a deep breath and stretch, creating tension in the hands, arms and chest region.

As you exhale, release the tension and, if you desire, allow your eyes to close.

Breathe normally on the next inhalation.

As you exhale, check the body for any remaining tension and "let go" of the tension on this exhalation.

THE BRIEF BODY SCAN TECHNIQUE

With a total of four normal breaths, body parts are relaxed sequentially within thirty to forty-five seconds. Allow your eyes to close if desired.

As you exhale from the first breath, allow your jaw to relax (let go, become heavy and loose).

As you exhale from the second breath, allow your shoulders to relax.

As you exhale from the third breath, allow your arms and hands to relax.

As you exhale from the fourth breath, allow your legs to relax.

The following references can broaden your knowledge base and provide practical tools for effective stress management. When selecting a reference, examine it carefully for strengths, weaknesses, and what could be of value to **you**.

RELAXATION TECHNIQUES

Allen, Roger J., & Hyde, Daniel. **Investigations in Stress Control.** Minneapolis, MN: Burgess Publishing Division, 1980. Pages 159-275.

Benson, Herbert. **The Relaxation Response.** New York: Avon Publishers, 1976.

Curtis, John D. & Detert, Richard A. **How to Relax: A Holistic Approach to Stress Management.** Palo Alto, CA: Mayfield Publishing Co., 1981.

Rosen, Gerald M. **The Relaxation Book.** Englewood Cliffs, N.J.: Prentice-Hall, Inc. 1977.

Walker, C. Eugene. **Learn to Relax: 13 Ways to Reduce Tension.** Englewood Cliffs, N.J.: Prentice-Hall, Inc., 1975.

STRESS THEORY AND INTERVENTION STRATEGIES

Dyer, Wayne. **Your Erroneous Zones.** New York: Avon, 1977.

Friedman, Meyer, & Rosenman, Ray. **Type A Behavior and Your Heart.** Greenwich, CT: Fawcett Crest Books, 1975.

Girdano, Daniel A. & Everly, George S. **Controlling Stress and Tension: A Holistic Approach.** Englewood Cliffs, N.J.: Prentice-Hall, Inc., 1979.

Jencks, Beata. **Your Body: Biofeedback at Its Best.** Chicago: Nelson-Hall Publishers, 1977.

Levi, Lennard. **Preventing Work Stress.** Reading, MA: Addison-Wesley Publishing Co., 1981.

Tubesing, Donald A. **Kicking Your Stress Habits.** Duluth, MN: Whole Persons Associates Inc., 1981.

BIBLIOGRAPHY

Curtis, John D., and Detert, Richard A. **How to Relax: A Holistic Approach to Stress Management.** Palo Alto, CA: Mayfield Publishing Co., 1981.

Girdano, Daniel A., and Everly, George S. **Controlling Stress and Tension: A Holistic Approach.** Englewood Cliffs, N.J.: Prentice-Hall, Inc., 1979

Healthy People: The Surgeon General's Report on Health Promotion and Disease Prevention. Washington, D.C.: U.S. Department of Health, Education, and Welfare, 1979.

Jencks, Beata. **Respiration for Relaxation, Invigoration, and Special Accomplishments.** Salt Lake City: Private printing, 1974.

Jencks, Beata. **Your Body: Biofeedback at Its Best.** Chicago: Nelson-Hall Publishers, 1977.

Prather, Hugh. **I Touch the Earth, The Earth Touches Me.** New York: Doubleday, 1972.

Ranta, P. **Exercises and Positions for the Finnish Olympic Ski Jumping Team.** Private conversation, September, 1977.

Shealy, C. Norman. **90 Days to Self Health.** New York: Dial Press, 1977.

White, John, and Fadiman, James. **Relax: How You Can Feel Better, Reduce Stress and Overcome Tension.** New York: Confucian Press, 1976.

MAIL ORDER INFORMATION

The following stress management materials are available from:

Coulee Press
P.O. Box 1744
La Crosse, Wisconsin 54602-1744

The Stress Management Card™

The Stress Management Card™ is a simple, easy-to-use, inexpensive biofeedback device based on the principle that tension causes constriction of the blood vessels and, thus, cold hands. As a person relaxes, the blood vessels on the surface of the extremities dialate, thus warming the hands and increasing the temperature. The Stress Management Card™ pictured below is a four-color card with temperature-sensitive liquid-crystal paper that responds to changing temperature by changing color. The card can be used by itself with the two stress management techniques on the back or with the coordinated materials. (i.e. the **Learn To Relax: A 14-Day Program** book and cassette tape.)

How To Use The Card

To monitor your level of tension and/or relaxation, place your thumb lightly on the black square for ten to twenty seconds. Then check the color directly under the thumb.

Black	Stressed
Red/Brown	Tense
Green	Calm
Blue	Relaxed

Use The Card To Check Your Tension Level

Periodically throughout the day, check your level of tension with the Stress Management Card™. If the card reads black or red, do a relaxation technique or an instant relaxation technique and, if you've mastered the skills, the card will change to green or blue.

Use the Card to Check Your Effectiveness at Relaxing

1. Check your level of tension prior to taking time to relax.
2. Perform selected relaxation techniques.
3. Check your level of relaxation after you have performed the techniques. With practice, most people can turn the card from black to blue in one

to five minutes if they have practiced the techniques outlined in **Learn to Relax: A 14 - Day Program.**

How to Order the Card

The durable, credit card-size Stress Management Card™ fits easily into a purse or wallet so that it is with you when you need it. For greater convenience, get several cards and keep one in the desk, in the car or at home so others can also benefit from its use. The card is also a great gift idea.

1 card	$3.95
2 - 3	2.95
4 - 9	2.50
10 - 19	2.25
20 - 29	2.00
30 - 49	1.75
50 - 100	1.60

Discounts available at higher amounts.

Books

Learn To Relax: A 14 - Day Program by John D. Curtis, Ph. D., and Richard A. Detert. Second edition. Coulee Press. 112 pages, 18 photographs.; 1985.

A simple, easy-to-follow book that teaches the basics

of relaxation. The book includes classroom-tested relaxation exercises, a fourteen-day log, motivational techniques, questions and answers, and a new chapter on instant relaxation techniques. The authors have over 19 years of experience between them teaching relaxation classes to students, educators, medical professionals, athletes, prison inmates, law enforcement agencies, and to people in business and industry. $4.95

How To Relax: A Holistic Approach to Stress Management by John D. Curtis, Ph.D., and Richard A. Detert. Mayfield Publishing Co. 222 pages, illustrated, 1981.

A detailed, self-care stress management book for people who want to do more than just cope with stress. This book includes more than 30 relaxation and sensory awareness exercises. Chapters on time management, the mind, communication skills, practical relaxation skills and the role of nutrition and exercise are included. This book is used in stress management and relaxation classes throughout the United States and in six foreign countries. $12.95

Cassette

The Learn To Relax cassette tape contains the four basic relaxation techniques from the book, **Learn To Relax: A 14 - Day Program.** The cassette can be used to lead you into a deeply relaxed state. Each exercise is followed by six to ten minutes of silence to allow adequate time to relax. .... **$8.95 each.**

To Prepare the Cassette for Use

Set the counter of the tape player at OOOO. Listen to the introduction on side one. Then run the tape player on fast forward speed until you find the beginning of the second exercise, "The Sequential Relaxation Exercise" (between 265 and 290 on the counter). Write the counter number on the cassette label so that you can find the second exercise with ease whenever you want it. Repeat this procedure for side two. Now that you can quickly locate each of the four exercises, you are ready to use the cassette for relaxation.

How to Use the Cassette

Select an exercise and listen to the cassette as it leads you into a relaxed state. At the end of each exercise, the narrator says, "Remain in this relaxed state until you are ready to terminate the exercise." From this point on you can come out of the relaxed state at any time. Exercises 1 and 3 are followed by six to eight minutes of silence before the narrator says that it is time to terminate the exercise. The six to ten minutes of silence following Exercises 2 and 4 end with the tape instead of the narrator's voice.

Stress Management Kit

Includes: **Learn To Relax: A 14 - Day Program** book
Learn To Relax: A 14 - Day Program cassette
Stress Management Card™

This is the only complete relaxation program available today. The combination of the book that describes and teaches the relaxation techniques, the cassette that leads you through the techniques, and the Stress Management Card™ that monitors your success at relaxation makes this a unique kit in stress management.

You save $1.90 when you buy all three.
A great gift idea!.................................... **$14.95**

MAIL ORDER FORM

		QUANTITY	AMOUNT

CARD
Stress Managment Card™ $3.95   _____   _____

BOOKS
Learn To Relax:
    A 14 - Day Program $4.95   _____   _____
Book w/Stress Management Card™ $7.95   _____   _____

How To Relax: A Holistic
    Approach to Stress
    Management $12.95   _____   _____

CASSETTE
Learn To Relax:
    A 14 - Day Program $8.95   _____   _____

STRESS MANAGEMENT KIT $14.95   _____   _____
Learn To Relax:
    A 14 - Day Program book
Learn To Relax: A 14 - Day
    Program cassette
Stress Management Card™

Total Price of Items   _____

Shipping and Handling $1.50
(not applicable to cards)

5% Sales Tax for Wisconsin Residents   _____

TOTAL   _____

Ship To: Name _____

      Address _____

      City _____ State _____ Zip _____

☐ Check or Money Order enclosed
☐ Please Charge my Mastercard account   MasterCard   VISA
☐ Please Charge my Visa account
Charge Account Number _____
My card expires _____

_____
Authorized Signature
Send your order to: Coulee Press, P.O. Box 1744
            La Crosse, Wisconsin 54602-1744
            (608) 788-6253

MAIL ORDER FORM

		QUANTITY	AMOUNT
CARD			
Stress Managment Card™	$3.95	_____	_____
BOOKS			
Learn To Relax:			
A 14 · Day Program	$4.95	_____	_____
Book w/Stress Management Card™	$7.95	_____	_____
How To Relax: A Holistic			
Approach to Stress			
Management	$12.95	_____	_____
CASSETTE			
Learn To Relax:			
A 14 · Day Program	$8.95	_____	_____
STRESS MANAGEMENT KIT	$14.95	_____	_____
Learn To Relax:			
A 14 · Day Program book			
Learn To Relax: A 14 · Day			
Program cassette			
Stress Management Card™			

Total Price of Items _____

Shipping and Handling $1.50
(not applicable to cards)

5% Sales Tax for Wisconsin Residents _____

TOTAL _____

Ship To: Name _____

Address _____

City _____ State _____ Zip _____

☐ Check or Money Order enclosed
☐ Please Charge my Mastercard account
☐ Please Charge my Visa account
Charge Account Number _____
My card expires _____

_____
Authorized Signature
Send your order to: Coulee Press, P.O. Box 1744
La Crosse, Wisconsin 54602-1744
(608) 788-6253